ISBN 978-94-011-8154-9 ISBN 978-94-011-8782-4 (eBook)
DOI 10.1007/978-94-011-8782-4

INTERNATIONAL BAR ASSOCIATION

MADRID CONFERENCE 1952

A COMMENTARY ON CONCILIATION OF DOMESTIC MATTERS

by

YOSHIMATSU TERASHIMA

CONTENTS

PREFACE

The task of conciliating domestic matters is certainly as difficult as it is holy. A deep-rooted trouble involving human affection and antipathy is a hard nut to crack by mere reasoning. There is, of course, no use influencing any interested parties imperatively or by sheer force. It is, indeed, a sacred job of sharing their fortunes to adjust their love of self, restore their former good-will and friendship, encourage their moaning souls and stabilize their livelihood. For that purpose, we should do our best to clarify the principle of law and new morality in guiding them, and to create the most appropriate terms of conciliation in persuading them. It is desirable to urge the conciliation commissioners, in their attempt to achieve a success, to give due deliberations and reflection besides they have a new sense and a keen insight. These qualities are, after all, only attainable when they have been fully trained, and have acquired experiences and novel ideas in the sphere of their activities.

In January 1950, I was ordered to give a lecture, for some newly appointed conciliation commissioners, on the subject of "Practical Methods of Domestic Conciliation." As, however, there was no publication available compiled by my predecessors on the practice and methods of domestic conciliation at that time, I was obliged to prepare a text of my own written entirely for the first time from my own experience, however scanty it was. That part of the description in this paper under caption of "Practical Business" is the whole text above referred to, which I admit to be quite insufficient because it was written in my leisure moments at home at night on account of my busy day-work in the office. This time again, I was asked to write, for the interest of some newly selected commissioners, a treatise on "Domestic Matters Conciliation." Fortunately I could avail myself of last consecutive Year-end and New Year holidays, and completed two new chapters on "Introduction" and "Legislation." I also made some additions to "Practical Business" in regard to "Standards of Conciliation" and "Conciliation Terms," with further supplementary notes on "Methods of Conciliation of Domestic Matters."

Inasmuch as the practice of domestic matters conciliation is a most important job, it is very difficult to describe it adequately. Feeling a great responsibility imposed upon my shoulder, I have to confess that I prepared this little pointer with great toil and application. I am afraid, however, that due to my mediocrity and immaturity I may have committed some inadvertent errors or dogmatic assertions. I am glad to say that after having shown this paper to my seniors I have obtained their approval on its publication.

Just full three years have elapsed since I engaged myself in the conciliation of domestic matters. But that holy mysterious land of treasure lies still unconquered beyond many rivers and mountains far in the distance. So we pilgrims must devote ourselves heart and soul to the steady progress of study. If this small work proves a milestone towards our destination, I shall be happier than I expected. Relying on good walkers in our party, I sincerely pray that they will before long reach the summit of the sacred mountain where they can command a grand view of the vast field of legislation. (Jan. 1951)

Chapter I. INTRODUCTION

2. Amendment to the Civil Code and Domestic Relations Law and the Family Court.

1) The New Constitution and Fundamental Concept of the Revised Civil Code and Domestic Matters Conciliation.

In Arts. 11 to 40, incl., of the New Constitution of Japan are stipulated the "Rights and Duties of the People." Among others, as regards dignity of individuals and the fundamental equality of the sexes, it proclaims the individual human rights in Art. 13, the equality of the people in Art. 14, and marriage and family life in Art. 24. Further in Art. 25 the right to live and the social welfare are defined, and in Art. 26 the right and duty to receive equal education. In the New Constitution we find the declarations: "Marriage shall be based only on the mutual consent of both sexes and it shall be maintained through mutual cooperation with the equal rights of husband and wife as a basis. With regard to choice of spouse, property rights, inheritance, choice of domicile, divorce and other matters pertaining to marriage and the family, laws shall be enacted from the standpoint of individual dignity and the essential equality of the sexes." (Art. 24)

Accordingly, the Civil Code, in pursuance of this fundamental idea, signified this principle in new Article 1–(2), while proper amendments were made in respect of 1) abolition of household, head of a family and family members; 2) freedom of marriage (Civil Code 737, 739); 3) equal rights of husband and wife (Civil Code 750, 760, 768, 818–3); 4) abolition of the right of succession to a house; 5) security of independent livelihood (distribution of property and spouse's right of succession), etc.

During the period from May 3, 1947 when the New Constitution became effective, to January 1, 1948 when the Amended Civil Code was put into force, the actual practice was done in accordance with the so-called "Law for Emergency Measures of the Civil Code," in the same manner as provided in the Amended Civil Code. Further in Article 1 of the Law of Adjudgment of Domestic Matters the principle of collective life of family members and relatives is stipulated thereby clarifying the fundamental idea of adjudgment and conciliation.

2) Nature of the Law of Adjudgment of Domestic Matters and the Mission of the Family Court.

Both the Law of Adjudgment of Domestic Matters and the Rules thereof are the procedural legislation enacted simultaneously with the Amended Civil Code in order to enforce these substantial statutes; and the Family Court (former Domestic Relations Court) was opened simultaneously chiefly in order to enforce these laws and regulations. In other words, by the enforcement of these legislations as well as by the administration of the Court, it is contemplated to purge families of feudalistic traits as early as possible, so that the actual life of the people may be improved democratically.

The Family Court was inaugurated on January 1, 1949 having combined the former Domestic Relations Court and the Juvenile Court, which had been operated as from January 1, 1948. The present Court is classified into two general divisions of the Domestic Relations Adjudgment Division and the Juvenile Adjudgment Division.

The former aims as its ideal to maintain the peace and happiness of families, and as its chief duty to conduct adjudgment and conciliation of domestic relations cases, while the latter has a mission to protect children and take care of their welfare. Thus the Family Court intends to maintain an integrated function of these two divisions for the purpose of promoting the effectiveness of the institution.

3. Organization of the Domestic Relations Adjudgment Division in the Family Court.

This division in the Family Court takes charge of the adjudgment and the conciliation of domestic relation cases. The judges who handle these cases are called the judges of domestic relation adjudgment. (Law Art. 2). A person who wishes to become the judge must have a professional experience of more than ten years as an appointed judge, public procurator, lawyer or university professor of jurisprudence, and must be an appointed judge (*saiban-kan*) qualified as a judge (*hanji*). A person who has been in the capacity of an assistant judge (*hanji-ho*) for more than five years may become a judge of domestic relations, if so designated by the Supreme Court as one authorised as a judge. (Art. 1 of the Law concerning Special Cases etc., of Authority of Assistant Judge).

1) Adjudgment.

Adjudgment is made jointly, as a rule, by a domestic matters judge or judges and councillors selected from among civilians who participate in the conference and express their opinions. (Law Art. 3, par. 3). As this treatise aims to relate the standards of domestic matters conciliation, details concerning adjudgment have been omitted here.

2) Conciliation.

Conciliation is, in principle, conducted by a Conciliation Commission organized by a domestic matters judge or judges and conciliation commissioners. (Law Art. 3–2). Councillors and conciliation commissioners are selected previously every year by the Family Court from among civilians who have high reputation and good knowledge and have a thorough worldly wisdom, and, in a specific case, the judge of domestic relations nominates councillors or conciliation commissioner each time an application is filed with the Family Court. (Law Art. 22–2). The domestic matters judge may, if he finds it necessary, appoint some other persons than mentioned above. (Law Art. 22–3)

3) Exclusion, Challenge and Evasion.

The system of exclusion, refusal and evasion is applicable to the judges of domestic matters, councillors and Family Court clerks as to their function, but it is not so with the counciliation commissioners because conciliation made on the agreement of the parties does not require such exceptions. (Law, 4; Code of Civil Procedure, 39, 44, 43).

4) Democratic Nature of the Family Court.

In the Family Court is set up the Court of Domestic Relations Committee with civilians of good knowledge as central force, who in response to inquiries, investigate and deliberate on the necessary matters concerning the over-all management of the Family Court. (Rule concerning the Court of Domestic Relations Committee). As related above, it is arranged that the Court of Domestic Relations Committee participates in the management and operation of the Family Court, the Councillors attend the adjudgment, and the Conciliation Commission take part in conciliation. This arrangement is most peculiar to the Family Court, which, we believe, characterizes the democratic constitution of the Court.

4. History of the Family Court.

First existance of the domestic matters adjudgment and conciliation dates far back to June 1922. They originated in a recommendation to the then government from the Speçial Legislation Council to the effect that "In order to settle family troubles amicably on the principle of morality instead of taking legal forms, it has been found essential to establish a certain special system." Then at a meeting of the Law Investigation Committee concerning the Court of Domestic Relations held on June 6, 1925 a resolution was adopted that "Adjudgment and conciliation of the cases concerning families shall be conducted by the Court of Domestic Relations," and further resolution was adopted on the matters of Councillors, Conciliation Commissioners and Conciliation Commission. Later on October 21, 1927 a bill of "the Adjudgment of Domestic Relations Act" was tentatively decided on. On July 1, 1939 the Personal Conciliation Law was enacted, by which it was made possible for the District Court to receive appeals for conciliation on "the cases concerning differences between family members or relatives and other domestic matters in general"; being in force until it was revised on Decembre 31, 1947.

Accordingly, the system of domestic matters conciliation now conducted by the Family Court is generally based on the former systems. Now that the fundamentals thereof have been replaced by the conception of the New Constitution, it may be said that an epoch-making reform has been effected in substance. That is to say, the guiding principle of domestic matters adjudgment and conciliation ought not to adhere to the "family system and the good manners and fine customs" of the former days. As aforementioned, the new guiding spirit must be "To maintain the peace and happiness of family and the sound collective living of family members and relatives on the principle of the individual dignity and the essential equality of the sexes." (Law 1).

CHAPTER II. PRACTICAL BUSINESS

Section 1. General Remarks.

5. Significance of Domestic Matters Conciliation.
Domestic matters conciliation means the legal procedures taken by the judge or Conciliation Commission in order to settle amicably the differences or troubles arising in family members or relatives under appropriate terms and conditions by making the parties concerned withdraw or concede their allegations.

6. Nature of Domestic Matters Conciliation.
Domestic matters conciliation is a system of settling differences so that the troubles relating to personal matters, family and relatives may be settled voluntarily by the parties through the coordination and assistance of judges and conciliation commission, the special government agencies. It is not a judicial trial in substance, but when

conciliation is formed and officially recorded in the protocol it will become as valid as the final and binding decree. (Law 21).

7. Method and Object of Domestic Matters Conciliation.

The object of domestic matters conciliation is to adjust and regulate egoisms or love of self (individual mental phenomena) of the parties concerned by law and morality (principles of collective life), in order to solve personal and family differences, aiming to bring forth a hope and sense of security to the family and the distressed members and relatives thereof.

8. Characteristics of Domestic Matters Conciliation.

Special feature of the domestic matters conciliation is to bring a peaceful and voluntary settlement of family and relational differences in a simple, speedy manner under proper terms and conditions, conducted in a closed session, by the judges and the civilian commissioners who have much worldly wisdom, learning, experiences and high virtues. Therefore, the conciliation has the following strong points and effects which symbolize the substance and character of the conciliation:

1) Principle of Simplicity.

Procedures are simple (Principle of simplicity). Oral application may be received. No particular documents whatsoever are required to be attached, except for the cases where divorce or other social personal matters are involved, a copy of census register is necessary, and in the case of divisional succession to property, an inventory, a will, etc. must be attached.

2) Saving of time, labour and cost is made possible. (Principle of official authority). The application fee is only thirty (30) yen (about $ 0,08) per conciliation case. Prompt settlement is available. These are the main reasons why it is popular with the general populace.

3) Principle of Closed door Session is adopted. Nobody other than the conciliation commissioners knows the details of the action.

4) Sympathetic assistance and advices are given with warm feelings and understanding. (Principle of personal appearance). So the parties can present real facts, and express their opinions and hopes freely. (Temple of Love).

5) Personal wilfulness or caprices are refrained. Friendly, polite and quiet talk is preferred.

6) Settlement will be made under the appropriate terms and conditions which are concretely defined in conformity to the principle

of collective life, because the standards for adjustment are based on law and morality.

7) Mutual agreement is the main point of settlement. Compromise is available. The parties may decide the case freely according to their own intentions.

8) Neither party will come out winning or losing the case. So no contention or serious opposition will be occasioned.

9) There is no chance of either party falling a victim to an extremely miserable condition.

10) In the course of a dispute the parties will be relieved from poverty. There is no fear of the party being forced to make concession owing to shrink from an unbearable burden of poverty before conciliation is reached.

11) Misapprehension on the part of the parties can be dispelled.

12) The parties do not retain any enmity or resentment against each other, because they feel grateful for the assistance and coordination afforded them by the Court.

13) It is possible to harmonize the alienated feelings and to restore the former friendship between the relatives.

14) Any settlement suited to the desire of the parties may be achievable even including the matters outside the dispute.

15) In an atmosphere of harmony and peace, the human rights may be extended, equality of the sexes be clarified, and the principle of democracy be pervaded to the people at large, and at the same time the justice of collective life may be elucidated and make them perform their obligations. (Protection of human rights and propagation of democracy).

16) Thus it is possible to safeguard against our private rights, concurrently bringing about good effects of the protection of children, the proper guidances of youth, the security of employment and protection of livelihood.

Section 2. Interpretation of Official Duties.

9. Primary Object is to Meet the People's Confidence and Expectation.

The people's recognition of the Family Court cannot yet be sufficient in quality and volume. It is, however, a fact that a large number of people have a deep confidence and great expectation in the Family Court. We must feel the seriousness of our responsibility and be prepared to meet their demands. After all, it means good conciliation executed promptly. It is natural for them to demand us to accelerate conciliation.

Accordingly, it is ruled to designate the date of first conciliation to take place within two weeks after acceptance of the case. This date, however, cannot but be fixed onesidedly by the Court on account of restrictions of an appointed period and inconvenience and difficulty in contact. If, therefore, either party finds it inconvenient to appear on the date first appointed by the Court, he is requested to inform a Court Clerk, as promptly as possible, of the fact by telephone or post-card so that the commissioners in charge of the case may be changed for other members. When one case coincides with the appointed hour of another case, or when the continuance date is interrupted, the Court Clerk must be notified of such fact. Of course, speediness is not always everything. Primary object is to conduct better conciliation. It is advisable, however, for us to care for the general demand of the people for the early settlement of dispute cases.

10. Service to the Populace and Constant Propagation.
We sometimes experience difficulties in appeasing the opponent of conciliation who has come to entertain antipathy against the claimant because of the latter's action being brought to the Family Court. May we think that such comes from the trend of thought still prevailing among the people to regard the Family Court a fearful and unapproachable place? If, however, we ourselves realize the duty of our public service, handling daily work kindly and politely with a peaceful mind, guiding them with morals and virtues in order to make settlement under fair conditions, then we have no doubt that some day the functions of the Family Court could be well understood and become familialized to the public. This also serves to popularize the Court. It is the very cardinal principle of making us really faithful public servants.

11. Functions of Reconciliation Adjusting Office.
The reconciliation adjusting office is a special organ of the Tokyo Family Court. The function of the office is to check attendance of the parties, their proxies or attorneys, interested persons and conciliation commissioners, to receive them, allot rooms, and to summon and contact the clerks who sit beside the judge and commissioners. This is an important place where is administered the daily handling of about sixty to eighty cases of conciliation. When the cases at issue are congested the room is so extremely crowded that the adjusting clerks find it difficult to receive people satisfactorily. But this adjusting

office, a sort of information desk, is likely to become an object of public criticism, and the members of its staff are instructed to be kind and polite in receiving all people, particularly the civilians. We eagerly desire the conciliation commissioners themselves to recognize this function of the office and co-operate with them so as to enable them to alleviate congestion and execute business punctually and speedily.

12. Interview and Written Communication with Interested Parties.
It is desired that all officials will grant interviews to parties concerned, without fail, at the Court only on the appointed date. To receive them at their own residence or to meet them in the Court on the day other than the appointed should be avoided, for such acts may perhaps be misunderstood by the other interested parties. Except for the cases where the judge's understanding has been obtained, they are required to meet the parties in the court on the day of conciliation, and to refrain from exchanging letters, etc. with them.

Even after the conclusion of a conciliation, when they were asked to meet them on visiting for reason of performance or pressing, such request must be referred to the competent judge whose instruction should be followed. In such a case the judge will summon the other party and advise him to perform his duty; and if other party desires to have the conditions of performance mollified, a new arrangement for application will be ordered, so that the direct and single-handed conference between the conciliation commissioners and interested parties must be avoided.

13. Closed door Sessions.
The closed door session system is one of the special major characters of domestic matters conciliation. Consequently, unless otherwise permitted, where necessary, as proxy, assistant or interested person of the party concerned, no relative or relation is allowed to be present at the court in session. (Law 6). It is the judge that permits the attendance of any observers.

14. Investigation of Records and Taking Notes.
Records of the case must be read through carefully before conciliation begins, and the outline thereof be taken note of for convenience's sake. If it takes a long time for reading, you must go to the court to read them thoroughly before the opening of a session. It is also essential to keep a full note of the parties' allegations, contents of evidence

and progress of the proceedings. Such records and data ought not to be divulged. When any interested party requests to peruse them such proposal must be consulted with the judge.

15. Filing of Case Cards.
In the Family Relations Section of the Supreme Court the filing card system was adopted as from January 1, 1951, by which classification is made according to Domestic Relations classes "A", and "B", Conciliation and Advices, etc. This card system serves for the compilation of statistical data as well as ready reference for judges and conciliation commissioners. When, therefore, no judge joins the session the commissioners are requested to cooperate in recording necessary facts thereon by themselves.

Section 3. General Procedures.

16. Disposition from Appearance to Commencement of Conciliation.
Upon appearing at Court on a fixed day you first go to the Adjusting Office, turn over your name-tablet, record time of attendance in the commissioner's duty card, impress seal, and ask the clerk to show your appearance in red circle mark. Then the commissioner who appeared first receives the records. When both parties arrived you go to a room designated by the clerk; and after arranging with the competent judge you may begin your work. If any other commissioners who are scheduled to join are absent, you may ask the judge's order instead of acting by yourself. Absence of appointed commissioner when both parties appeared at fixed time is a disgrace to the court, you must always be punctual.

17. Opening, Progress and Conclusion of Conciliation.

1) Legally speaking, conciliation starts on accepting a case.

a) Both of interested parties are first admitted to a room, identified, and their vocation, assets, income, and other required items are checked and recorded in the card.

b) Simple explanation on the object and special characters of the conciliation system is given.

c) The parties are alternately admitted to the room and their actual conditions of the case are heard.

d) When the judge does not participate in the session, the conciliation commissioners have to report the proceedings to the judge, and the course of conciliation must necessarily be decided on at the Commission's conference jointly with judge.

e) Examination of facts and taking evidence must always be made in the presence of the judge.

f) The interested parties' allegation and insistance should be regulated by law and morality and they must be induced to compromise or concede on a certain line of propriety.

g) When session is to be continued, new date is to be fixed upon consultation with the judge.

h) Any change in the course of conciliation and decision on conciliation terms shall be made at the Commission's joint conference with the judge.

i) Resolution of the Conciliation Commission shall be adopted by the opinion of majority of the commissioners. (Reg. 135)

j) Conferences of the Conciliation Commission shall be kept secret. (Reg. 136, Law 28).

2) Formation of Conciliation, Conciliation by Adjudgment. Compulsory Conciliation, Withdrawal, Unsuccessful Conciliation and Improper Application for Conciliation.

a) When an agreement reached between both parties is recorded in the protocol (Commissioners must, as a rule, sign the protocol when judge prepared conciliation terms and declares them aloud), the conciliation is deemed to have been formed, and such statement shall have the same effect as the finally binding decree. (A final adjudgment for the cases class "B"). (Law 21).

b) But the above rulings are different in the case of conciliation by adjudgment and compulsory conciliation as provided for in Arts. 23 and 24 of the Law hereof. (Law 25). In the event of any objection being raised within two weeks such validity is lost, and if no objection is raised it shall have the same effect as the finally binding decree.

c) In either case where there was the same effect as the final decree, the party concerned may resort to compulsory execution by virtue of the said protocol taken as title of obligation.

d) In cases where the applicant presented a written statement of withdrawal, irrespective of reason whether the case has been settled satisfactorily in substance or the opponent was in default or the conciliation was unsuccessful, the case shall be concluded. In this case the withdrawal must be shown reason of withdrawal, i.e., "Withdrawn on satisfactory settlement".

e) In the event of the case having been tentatively disposed of with a later date for conciliation designated because of absence of both parties, and a protocol was prepared with a notation relating "No conciliation shall be made," after having served summons and notification, the case shall be deemed to have been terminated.

f) When conciliation was unsuccessful, the case will be closed after protocol has been prepared as a failure, but as to the case class "B" it is presumed that application for adjudgment had been made at the time of applying for conciliation.

g) For any improper conciliation application with an unjust purpose (Reg. 138) a protocol shall be made to the effect that no conciliation will be made and the case may be concluded as final.

18. Acceleration and Settlement of Conciliation.
It is advisable that any conciliation ought to be accelerated smoothly, and no chance must be lost to bring the case to a successful settlement as early as possible, and no case shall be unreasonably retained intact. For this purpose the judges and conciliation commissioners, in one body, must always cooperate with each other. As the judges have too many cases on hand at present they are unable to attend to all proceedings every time. Accordingly, when the conciliation commissioners find it necessary to discuss as to the change in the course of conciliation on account of new allegations put forth by the interested parties, they must confer with the judges on the subject. Needless to say, the conciliation terms shall always be decided upon with a joint conference with the judge.

19. Protocols to be Signed by Conciliation Commissioners.
Minutes of proceedings to be signed by conciliation commissioners may be classified into the conciliation procedure protocol, the successful conciliation protocol, the special conciliation protocol as defined in Art. 23 of the Law of Adjudgment of Domestic Matters, the conciliation protocol of adjudgment to be made in place of the protocol as defined in Art. 24 of the same Law, and the protocol for postponement or change of conciliation date. When conciliation was decided as a success or a failure, the commissioners are requested to sign necessary documents in the presence of a competent Clerk of the Court.

20. Disposition after Termination of Conciliation until Leaving the Court.
When leaving the Court after attending conciliation, you are requested to return the records to the Adjusting Office and to enter leave hour in the attendance card. This record will be a basis for payment of attendance allowances.

Section 4. Special Procedures.

21. Representatives or Attorneys-at-Law.
Conciliation requires interested parties to appear in person. (Reg. 5). Attorneys other than lawyers are permitted to appear only in cases where the principal is too old or ill or when he lives in an outlying district. Reasons why the principal is required to appear in person are that the principal himself is most acquainted with the actual circumstances of the case and that the agreement by the parties is reached by the concession and compromise of principals and especially their resolute decision is often essential.

If, however, one desires to delegate one's powers to a lawyer there is no ground for refusal, because the latter's assistance and proper conciliation are required for a fair and proper conciliation. But even when a lawyer is in attendance, if the principal's personal statement is desired, lawyer may be asked to leave the room. When there was an application for permission of attendance of a lawyer or when a lawyer alone appeared instead of the principal, the fact must be notified immediately to the judge. (Reg. 5).

22. Valuation of Real Estate and Taking Evidence.
In order to create the "concretely appropriate standard" necessary for the settlement of the case it is required to grasp the truth of facts. So it becomes necessary to examine witnesses or order the assistance of experts. If, for instance the parties do not agree with each other as to the value of movables, immovables or securities, valuation of the same shall always be decided upon by an expert sent by the judge's order. Examination of facts and taking evidence are conducted by the judge *ex officio*. (Law 7, 8). In the case of above procedure the judge must be consulted.

23. Cases concerning Domiciles outside Jurisdiction.
Reason why the Court accepts an application in respect of a case in which the opponent's domicile does not fall under its jurisdiction is that there exist special circumstances in which the applicant is too aged, ill or in poverty. Therefore, when the opponent himself or his attorney appeared, the fact must be instantly notified to the judge and when procedures continue to another day the opponent will be ordered to appear in person on the appointed day making him sign his acknowledgment.

24. Order of Emergency Measures.
If, on the cases of divorce, support of family and division of property succeeded to, the opponent is likely to conceal or squander such property, or when the appellant is in an extreme difficulty due to hard living and illness, the judge's advice must be sought for emergency measures in application of provisions of Article 133 of the Regulations of Adjudgment of Domestic Matters.

25. Exflux Procedure for Receiving Food Allocation.
In case where the opponent does not take procedure intentionally for the exflux of the appellant, if the judge of domestic matters or the Conciliation Commission finds it unjust and improper, they may order one of the parties to take necessary procedures for exflux as a necessary disposition prescribed in Art. 133 of the Regulations of the Adjudgment of Domestic Matters. In case where the opponent does not take any procedure by an appointed date under the order, if the appellant living separately applied to the head of village, town or ward of city where other party resides, submitting a copy of the order, for the exflux of other party, the head of the said municipal office is authorized to deliver a certificate of exflux and cancel the name of such person from the official pass-book for staple food consumers in the said area, and take necessary measures to suspend allocation of staple foods. (Instruction No. 8085 of the President of the Food Agency to the Prefectural Governors).

26. Welfare Disposition.
As to assistance of livelihood, superintendence of child, medical treatment and other dispositions in the cases of divorce, support of living and upbringing of child, if it is found necessary to negotiate with the Child Welfare Official, Child Welfare Station or Welfare Commissioner the fact must be instantly referred to the judge. In order to keep close contact between the Family Court and Government Agencies connected with social relief work a monthly meeting of the welfare affairs bodies is held. Lectures and inspection trips are scheduled to take place from time to time. We suggest it advisable that further legislation be enacted to promote the activities of organs prescribed in the Rules of the Mental Health Law and the Livelihood Protection Law.

27. Hearing the Opinions of Minors.
In cases where parents have children under fifteen years of age in the

case of their divorce, the minors' opinion must be necessarily consulted when deciding on the divorce of parents, the superintendence of children and parental power.

28. Disposition against the Absentees.
As to disposition taken in case of absence of interested party or parties, there are measures such as notice of imposing non-penal fines, sending competent police officers for admonition, conducting conciliation on the spot and compulsory conciliation. The judge must be consulted in this case. (Code of Civil Procedure 277–2, 278, Constitution 32, Family Court Law 24).

29. Place of Payment Set forth in the Conciliation Terms.
We often have many such cases where after conciliation is formed the obligee applies to the Court for assistance to urge the obligator to perform his duty as the former neglects to pay consolation money and expenses of education. This usually is due to the facts that their former ill feelings have not been removed, trouble of remitting by money-order or handing money in person, uneasiness about direct delivery of money between the parties, disputes as to the issue of recept, etc. Under the circumstances, it is advisable for them to designate the Family Court as place of payment in the conciliation terms until the Court sets up a special depository bank or the deposit trust system.

30. Recommendation to Relief Committee of Lawyer's Association.
In case of unsuccessful conciliation, decision of non-conciliation, or withdrawal thereof, if either of the parties desiring to continue suit or other litigation is (*a*) unable to employ lawyer on account of poverty, (*b*) in need of a suitable lawyer recommended, (*c*) too poor to hire a lawyer by himself and wishes for recommendation of lawyer who is willing to serve at low cost, the chief of the Domestic Relations Section of the Court will comply with his request by introducing him to the Relief Committee of the Lawyers' Association, and in that case it is requested to apply to the judge.

Section 5. Standards of Domestic Matters Conciliation.

31. Standards of Domestic Matters Conciliation.
It goes without saying that the standards of domestic conciliation is the principle of collective life with law and morality as its foundation.

Deep and hard are the feuds among blood relations. In some cases not only can rights and obligations and even sense of morality hardly solve the problem, but nor could affinity of parents and child or love of husband and wife prevail very much. There is, therefore, no other means but to settle their differences under most just and appropriate terms in accordance with the circumstances of individual cases after taking into consideration the details of the dispute, personal character of the parties concerned, relation of their education and property, condition of business, and circumstances in which the family, family members and relatives are situated. We cannot but say that the direct and synthetically proper standards applied is, therefore, "the tangible propriety" itself.

1) Legislation and Principle for Conciliation Standards.

a) Important Legislation.

Substantial laws and ordinances specially necessary for study in domestic matters conciliation are: provisions of Chapter 3 of the New Constitution prescribing rights and obligations of the people; the fundamental human rights in Articles 11 to 40 inclusive, individual rights of the people in Art. 13, equality of the people in Art. 14, personal liberty in Art. 18, freedom of thought and conscience in Art. 19, marriage and family life in Art. 24, people's right to live and social relief facilities in Art. 25, and right and duty to receive education in Art. 26; General Provisions of Arts. 1 and 1–(2) in Book I of the Civil Code, relatives in Book IV, succession in Book V; and other laws and ordinances relating to labour, education and welfare.

Total number of conciliation cases handled so far by the Tokyo Family Court and classified by nature of cases may be shown as follows (in percent): divorces 39, dissolution of informal marriage 20, support of family members or relatives 7, non-existence of parent-child relation 7, cohabitation of husband and wife 4, division of inherited property 2, legal acknowledgement $1\frac{1}{2}$, restoration of property 1, and others 18. From the above it will be seen that special study is required on the Civil Code, particularly on provisions concerning marriage, divorce, relation of parents and child, parental power, support of family members and relations, heir and validity of succession.

b) "Individual Dignity" and "Essential Equality of the Sexes".

On "Individual Dignity" and "Essential Equality of the Sexes" the New Constitution proclaims individual human rights provided for in Art. 13, equality of the people in Art. 14, and marriage and family life in Art. 24. These rights are also stipulated in Art. 1–(2) of the Amended Civil Code; and in Art. 1 of the Law of Adjudgment of Domestic Matters. The above cited provisions are certainly the "iron rules" as standards of domestic matters conciliation.

c) "Principle of Respecting Family Life".

To say nothing of the individual dignity and equality of the sexes, it is natural for us to follow justice and the principle of friendship, respect and affection and cooperation among ourselves in order to maintain the peace and happiness of the family life and sound collective life of relatives. In the New Constitution, however, there is no stipulation as to how to make our family life peaceful and harmonious. It is, therefore, most appropriate that neither the express provision in Art. 730 of the Civil Code reading "Blood relatives of lineal ascendant and the relations living together shall help each other" nor the provision in latter part of Article 1 of the Law of Adjudgment of Domestic Matters reading "the object is to maintain peace of family and sound collective life of relatives" denies the "principle of respecting the family life". Excessive individualism in the family ought to be adjusted after all.

d) "Principle of Faith and Trust".

There are newly prescribed provisions in Art. 1 of the Amended Civil Code: "all private rights shall be exercised in conformity with the public welfare"; "The exercise of rights and performance of obligations shall be done faithfully and in accordance with the principle of trust"; "No abuse of rights is permitted". This ruling signifies that morality should exist in legislation, too, and this spirit must always govern the conciliation of domestic matters.

e) Laws and Ordinances Relating to Conciliation.

The laws and ordinances regarded as necessary for, and relation to, the conciliation of domestic matters are as follows:

The Constitution, Pension Law, Civil Code, Law No. 74 of 1947 concerning Temporary Measures for the Civil Code, Ordinances, Nationality Law, Commercial Code, Law of Bills, Law on Cheques, Bankruptcy Law, Law concerning Guaranty of Social Status, Leasehold Land Law, Leased Building Law, Law Providing Temporary Measures concerning the Leasehold Land and Leased Building in the Cities Damaged by War, Criminal Code, Juvenile Law, Labour Standards Law, Trade Union Law, Labour Relations Adjustment Law, Unemployment Insurance Law, Employment Security Law, Fundamental Law of Education, School Education Law, Social Education Law, Social Undertakings Law, Social Welfare Commissioner Law, Eugenic Protection Law, Medical Treatment Law, Mental Health Law, Child Welfare Law, Livelihood Protection Law, Staple Food Management Law, Ordinance concerning the Control of Land and House Rent, Agricultural Land Adjustment Law, Owner Farmers Establishment Special Measures Law, Immovables

Registration Law, Family Registration Law, Law for Adjudgment of Domestic Matters, Rules of Adjudgment of Domestic Matters, Rule of Adjudgment of Special Domestic Matters, Rule of Juvenile Trial, Law of Procedure in Non-Contentious Matters, Law of Procedure in Personal Matters, Law for Conciliation, Various Tax Laws, etc.

Besides these laws and regulations, there are the Customary Law and Law of Justice. Custom and justice must not always be excluded as feudalistic remains. We still consider as ruling custom and justice such common practices in marriage engagement, contract of marriage of consent, and succession of religious service and festivals in honor of ancestors. Furthermore, judicial precedents, precedents of adjudgments and conciliation in the Family Court, and instructions and answers of the Supreme Court and the Attorney General's Office, etc. are useful materials for the interpretation of laws and ordinances.

2) Morality.

New morality for family members and relatives has its source in the fundamental human rights prescribed in the Constitution, and particularly is based on the principle of individual dignity and the essential equality of the sexes. Therefore, any good manners and customs which are contrary to this fundamental principle must be abolished. Such sense of superiority as enjoyed the head of a family and the husband must be abandoned and an excessive leaning to individualism ought to be remedied.

Although we admit that many of the Japanese families cannot support themselves economically, it is true that they live a peaceful and happy collective life sharing fortunes, being endowed with virtues of mercy and protection, compassion and respect for the aged, love and harmony, friendship and mutual concession, cooperation and assistance, modesty and perseverance, honesty and diligence. This way of living is, in itself, a fine life of morality, which, we are proud to say, is founded on the admirable Japanese tradition and the centuries-old culture highly estimated by the peoples of the world. Certainly it is necessary to give our deep consideration to the building of new morals and the guidance of their practices. A heavy responsibility is said to be placed on the conciliation commissioners.

3) "Principle of Tangible Propriety".

"Things which are not flat rattles" — this means one demands equity. "Unsettled mind wavers" — it means everything requires stabilization. Tangible propriety is an integrated reasonableness which controls such equity and stabilization. Therefore, tangible propriety is the supreme fundamental principle as well as the sacred legislation. It is not originally separated from law and morality, but rather embraces or takes them, and further it is created and formed by them. It must be noted that "Tangible propriety" is not a vague, uncertain common sense at all.

Section 6. Conciliation Terms.

32. Creation and Kinds of Conciliation Terms.

1) Creation of "Concretely Appropriate Terms of Conciliation". Terms of domestic matters conciliation must be concretely just and proper in conformity to the contents of the case at issue. In other words, they are determined by the aforesaid "tangible propriety", and are created and formed by the intellect and good knowledge of adjudgment judges and conciliation commissioners. For instance, as to the amount of consolation money, subsistence allowance and divided property, it is natural that the amount of money or property are not always uniformly assigned to each of the parties, because it varies according to physical condition, age, occupation, assets, income, position, social standing, etc. of the interested persons. If, however, such amount of money is fixed perfunctorily and excessively out of balance compared with other cases, such conciliation can never be called a good one. So the commissioners are requested to cooperate with one another in their study on standards of conciliation and other methods of common interest concerning their daily work.

Any items of illegal effect, though inserted in the protocol, have no legal validity. Any doubt as to legal points must be referred to the judge without reserve. However, any commissioner who is not familiar with very simple rules and regulations will not only be despised by the parties but may perhaps be in danger of making an unappropriate conciliation. Fortunately, we see, since last summer (1951), a regular meeting being held on each first Saturday of the month at one o'clock p.m. to discuss and study matters on everyday work, and also a monthly meeting for study of various cases held on each third Tuesday of the month under guidance of the Family Relations Bureau of the Supreme Court to make study on domestic matters and juvenile relation cases. All interested officials are recommended to join each of these meetings.

2) Kinds of Conciliation Terms.

Conciliation terms may be classified into the following four general groups according to their contents:

a) Terms concerning Rights and Obligations.

Let us cite a few instances here. "The parties concerned effected their divorce this day"; "The parties concerned confirmed this day that they dissolved their informal contract of marriage on consent and hereafter there shall exist no social relation of husband and wife between them"; or "It is adjudged that the appellant, named Hana, shall take over 3-year old eldest son, Chotaro, born between the two parties, and take care of and bring up the child, and the parental power over him shall rest on the mother". Other terms of conciliation will be concerning the consolation money, time and manner of payment and delivery of property due to division of property, negligence clauses, decision of obligee and obligator to support family members, extent and method of supporting them, etc.

b) Terms concerning Manner of Living.

Here is an example: "Persons interested in the case, named Taro Kono and Hana Kono, (husband and his wife who is elder sister of opponent husband), shall take over an interested person, named Tome Otsuno, (mother of the opponent husband) on and after February 1, 1951, and shall, until the party concerned requests the said Tome to return and live together with him, take care of the old mother and support her and bear all expenses to be incurred therefor", and other matters concerning education of child or children, medical treatment, etc., involved in the case.

c) Terms concerning Warning Instructions.

To show an example: "The parties concerned shall respect and love each other, be diligent in their vocational work, educate their child or children and make a happy and peaceful home".

d) Terms concerning Payment of Costs.

Payment of fees for expert opinions and other charges concerning the conciliation must be fixed as to the party responsible therefor.

Section 7. Methods of Conciliation.

33. Clear-headed Insight and Absence of Prejudice.

The Japanese sayings go: "Clouds of a mirror must be wiped off before one gets good reflection", and "When water ripples, reflected shadows move". It frequently happens that some persons who look very handsome and intelligent prove to be haughty and obstinate, while others who are ugly and unmindful of their appearances are modest, unassuming and full of cooperative spirit. There are such persons who are rich in worldly wisdom, self-complacent, smooth-tongued and insidious. Some others are gentle and meek but honest, naive, and even dull-witted but pure-hearted. Some are self-indulgent, careless, insincere and frivolous, while others are rich and humble, and poor but incorruptible.

Therefore, in order to give a good judgment for measures to be taken after recognizing all facts involved, it is necessary for conciliation commissioners to have not only a new sense and a keen insight but also deep mediation, profound reflection and immaculate knowledge. Such disposition made generously to the rich and powerful and strictly to the poor and weak shall never be permitted.

34. Method of Conciliation and Preparedness. Although the Law of the Adjudgment of Domestic Matters and the Rules thereof have minutely prescribed the legal procedures concerning conciliation, no provision is found with regard to such method of persuasion and adjustment that leaves nothing to be desired for the settlement of family disputes by mollifying the feeling and compromising the allegations of the parties. Conciliation, to my thinking, can never be attained by *finesse* or eloquence after all. The secret of conciliation is, in the main, to induce them patiently until they become convinced of its result, by giving them a chance to reflect on a footing of moral principle and by caring after them with a kinsman's heart with tenderness and understanding. Some serious and complicated troubles intertwined with human affection and antipathy could hardly be settled by law and reason alone. A successful conciliation chiefly depends upon both parties' utmost confidence in the conciliators to whom they come willingly with abated excitement, softened feelings, awakened responsibility as well as with a sense of reflection and concession. In order to move them in such a manner there is no alternative but to approach them with good judgment, enthusiasm, sincerity and high virtues. Especially, it is essential that conciliation terms be very tangibly fair and appropriate, and must be convincing to all from objective points of view. We cannot but rely, in the long run, on the sterling character and adequate knowledge of commissioners in order to secure a good conciliation.

35. Attitude and Readiness for Conciliation. The final object of domestic matters conciliation is to stabilize the family life and give it a gleam of hope. So that it is required to investigate beforehand into the condition of a family as well as the economic and moral life of each member of the family besides the actual circumstances of the parties and the case involved. In attempting a conciliation it is always necessary to create a congenial atmosphere among those sitting around a table. Try to clear the misunderstanding of the parties by taking into consideration not only the interests of the parties but also the happiness of the family and the entire

members of the relatives. In order to remove resentment and enmity from their mind you ought to be patient and generous talking to them kindly and politely. When you sit with arrogant and insolent persons, be cautious about your own language and persuade them insinuatingly, and they will come to appreciate your kindness and willingly obey to your counsel. Be aware that force and power have always reactions. Kindness to another person seems to be thoroughly appreciated when you give it on a religious conviction.

36. Expedient of Persuasion and Compromise on Ethics and Religion.

Conciliation of domestic matters is to protect, by means of mediation and compromise, private rights and serves to promote the effects of juvenile protection, proper guidance of youth, security of employment and livelihood protection. So the conciliation itself may justly be called to assume a special character functioning as an executing organ of social policies for education, relief and welfare in a broad sense. In persuading the parties in conciliation, you might dwell upon, in accordance with the personality of the parties and the contents of the alleged case, the virtues of unselfishness, fortitude and accumulation of good deeds, or emphasize the theory of education and the practice of morals. Of course, you may be free to inquire into the faith of the parties and try to lead them properly by preaching on the Mercy of Buddhism or on the Love of Jesus Christ. The only thing to which I wish to call your attention here is that such elucidation should not exceed a certain limit as an expedient to reach a successful conciliation. Because if such an effort aiming at thorough correction and reformation as well as induction to religious beliefs go to the extremes out of enthusiasm on the part of conciliators, there is a danger of retarding the settlement of the problem and arousing the antipathy of the parties concerned.

37. Spirit of Sharing Difficulties.

It is most desirable for the conciliation commissioners to be persons of good learning, far-sightedness, wordly wisdom, gentle and generous character, and fluent speech. It is, however, particularly desired that woman commissioners be tender-hearted and kind enough to share worries and difficulties with the poor distressed people, and clever and resourceful enough to offer help, even with tears, to those whether they are women abandoned by husband, or men forsaken by wife, or girls ill-treated by their mother-in-law.

38. Don't Blame Their Sins and Errors.
We have to deal frequently with some of those people who are faithless and self-indulgent, lazy and neglectful and addicted to drunken frenzy always threatening others with violence, to such an extent that they forget their parental responsibility, neglect their duty as husband, or fail to offer their filial services. When we, however, trace such deviations carefully, we find some motives or remote causes which have driven them to such pitiful conditions out of their individual character, predisposition, heredity, or accursed surroundings. Therefore, it is not advisable to blame their sins and errors, but it is right to understand and sympathize with them so as to make them correct their behaviour and walk in the path of virtue. A single heart of love and mercy will certainly make the parties feel easy and lead the conciliation to a successful end.

39. Avoid Discussion and Talk with Friendliness.
It is sometimes necessary to argue with the parties about conciliation with the morality of collective life, but I suggest that you had better refrain from making discussions. I hope that woman conciliators do their best to show their special points of excellence by addressing them kindly, so that they may be deeply moved and led to accede to an amicable settlement.

40. Synthetic Judgment Covering the Whole Range.
In order to create a "tangible propriety" necessary for the settlement of the case, you must determine it by confirming individual facts and integrating them into an entirety upon which your observation is based. It is wrong to stick to a single point of fact being influenced by your own emotion thereby disregarding propriety under the principle of morality. We should always cultivate the power of judgment lest it should become commonplace and too delicate.

41. Women's Imploration for Understanding.
Women would say that none but women can truly understand the mind of a woman. Should a conciliation commissioner answer carelessly with his subjective and wilful feelings, to the petition of a woman party, it is sure to arouse her antipathy and cause an unnecessary trouble in consequence. So you must be very careful in your expression as it has an important bearing on the fate of a conciliation. It is needless to say, however, that no woman commissioner is present merely to take a woman's side.

42. Dismissal of Children.
Infants and children, regardless of their age, shall be dismissed, as far as possible, when their parents sit for a conciliation. In the presence of children an examination of parents' misdeeds and admonition and warning against parents must be tabooed, for such acts are likely to impair the dignity of parents and make the youngsters feel a sadness of disillusion, which may cause the deliquency of children and result in rupture of a peaceful and happy home life.

43. Feudalistic Families to be Regenerated.
We see some such lamentable cases like this: The appellant, an old wife, complains against her opponent husband who is an "après-guerre" of eccentricities and despot of feudalistic idea. She comes in a wretched condition seeking redress for the great sacrifice she offered denying her own self for the sake of her parents, husband and children, because she thought women's fortitude as one of their highest virtues. In such a case you must lay particular stress on the fundamental principle of individual dignity and equality of the sexes, and endeavour with a strong will to regenerate their family with a new gleam of hope by remedying the feudalistic control in the family.

44. Security of Independent Livelihood.
The fact that the New Civil Code provides for an equal opportunity to both sexes for the acquisition of property in divorce and succession comes fundamentally from the stipulation in the Constitution to the effect that all people shall have the right to maintain the minimum standards of wholesome and cultured living. Accordingly, when we decide the distribution of property and the division of estate we must realize this great spirit of the law.

45. Emergency Measures for Support of Family Members.
It is noteworthy that the number of cases concerning the support of family members or relatives ranks third in the list of total number of domestic conciliation cases handled by our Court. In pursuance of the idea of provision in Article 25 of the Constitution, the Livelihood Protection Law stipulates that the government shall provide necessary protection and guarantee the minimum standards of living for the people in poverty in conformity to the extent of poverty, shall encourage their self-supporting, and that such minimum standards of living shall be so fixed as to enable them to maintain a wholesome and cultured living. But in order to receive protection under the Livelihood

Protection Law it is required first to receive support from the person who is legally responsible for it as prescribed in the Civil Code as well as the aid defined in another law. The Civil Code, however, provides that the child is bound only to support his parents to such extent that he is able to offer his extra cost of living, and when no agreement is or cannot be reached between the parties as to the extent and method of support, the Family Court makes an adjudgment. For such reason, applications for adjudgment and conciliation are filed with the Court. As, however, the Livelihood Protection Law provides that it shall not preclude any necessary protection in case of imminent causes, it is desired to consult with the judge in this case. With regard to the cases concerning the support of family members or relatives, we must endeavour to maintain and promote the fine traditional custom of our country to respect and protect old persons.

46. Protection of Children and Checking of Divorces.
The number of divorce conciliation cases occupies the foremost position among all cases handled by our Court. We see, however, such cases where due to divorce mother and children who have been receiving aid under the Livelihood Protection Law are still at a loss on account of their illness. Some children are also treated cruelly by their stepmother. This misery comes from the irresponsible divorce of parents at the sacrifice of their children. We feel great concern about the future delinquency of such children. Any divorce without security of life shall be checked and regulated as far as possible. Such a frivolous idea of regarding emancipation of woman as divorce must be corrected.

47. Children's Charter and Protection of Children.
On May 5, 1951, the Children's Day established for the first time in Japan, an epoch-making code called "Children's Charter" was instituted. Children have the hope and responsibility to build up next generation. A most careful consideration should be given them for their protection. The following is an outline of the Draft Charter for Children:

EXTRACT OF CHILDREN'S CHARTER

1. All children shall be equally respected as individuals and be afforded the security of living and loving protection.

2. Sweet home and culture shall be maintained for children, and any children who are not blessed with their homes shall be given a homelike protection.
3. All parents shall be conscious of their responsibility for their children and shall have proper affection, knowledge and technical experience for the upbuilding of children.
4. Individuality of children must be cultivated and they shall be taught the responsibility and actions as a member of the society.
5. Children shall enjoy sunshine and fresh air and be given proper nourishment.
6. Children shall be protected from all kinds of diseases and calamities.
7. Children shall be afforded opportunities to receive culture and vocational guidance correspondent to their individuality and ability.
8. All children shall not be hampered from the growth of their body and mind nor shall be deprived of opportunities to receive education because of hard labour, nor shall they be robbed of the enjoyment of life which is indigenous to them.
9. Children shall be protected by law against all evil deeds such as cruelty, ill-treatment and non-interference.
10. Children impaired of mental and physical functions shall receive proper medical treatment and education.

48. Immediate Help Necessary to Restore Lost Happiness.
Failures in marriage come frequently from the parents' ignorance of law and morality of a new era concerning the marriage. In such a case, the parents must be summoned and guided under new Constitutional rulings: "Marriage shall be based only on the mutual consent of both sexes", and "Marriage shall be maintained through mutual cooperation with the equal rights of husband and wife as a basis." This happens because some parents who still stick to an old established custom think that in proposal of marriage for their sons and daughters they can enforce their discretion and make the life of the newlyweds absolutely submitted to the will of the parents. But as any assistance in conciliation will hardly be successful when the matter gets entangled, it is necessary to conciliate both parties earnestly so as to reach a speedy conclusion.

49. Best Efforts and Unsuccessful Conciliation.
Despite that the conciliation commissioners are right in their judg-

ment on the facts, kind and polite in their persuasion and the methods, and terms and conditions are just and proper enough, the parties would not be moved and refuse to concede in all points. Conciliation is really a hard job. However knotty the problem involving mutual hatred may be, if we are prepared to do our best to the very last in in order to reach a successful settlement, we should never be dragged along by the selfishness of either party, yield to his obstinacy, nor give a tacit permission for the unappropriate terms agreed upon between the parties themselves, and at the same time we must uphold and carry through a conciliation course already fixed by the Conciliation Commission in order to make a correct and proper conciliation. For that purpose, we cannot help admitting an unsuccessful conciliation.

50. Wits and Successful Conciliation.
It often happens that some parties who did not make any concession because of their self-complacency and obstinacy would suddenly change their mood and come to assume a compromising attitude on the spur of the moment when some interesting fun or joke is uttered by a conciliator. It is therefore desirable for the commissioners to be placid enough to be chatty and humourous so as to produce a very congenial atmosphere among those sitting together at a table in order to lead the parties to an amicable settlement of the case in friendly terms. To read them a lecture disregarding the changing mood and intentions of the parties all the time out of impetuosity for a speedy conclusion should be avoided lest such should cause us to miss a chance to arrive at a successful conciliation.

Chapter III. LEGISLATION

Section. 1. Jurisdiction.

51. Jurisdiction over Domestic Matters Conciliation.

1) Jurisdiction Based on Legal Matters (Objects of Conciliation). The Family Court conducts conciliation for legal actions concerning personal affairs and other general cases relating to domestic matters, but the adjudgment cases as prescribed in Article 9, item 1, class "A" of the Law hereof, shall be excepted from this rule. (Law 17). As to the so-called "B" cases they can be applied for either conciliation or adjudgment at the option of the applicant, and the Court may submit a case "B" applied for adjudgment to the conciliation at any time.

(Law 11). The conciliation ended in failure is naturally transferred to adjudgment (Law 26), so the result will be the same as if it were applied for adjudgment from the beginning. The provision of Article 17 of the Law hereof has the same meaning as Article 1 of the former Law of Adjudgment of Personal Matters which prescribes as "The case concerning dispute between family members or relatives and other domestic matters in general ...." So that this provision may be applied with necessary modifications to the following cases although persons involved are not the blood relations: cases concerning matters between husband and wife of marriage on mutual consent; non-performance of marriage previously engaged; cases concerning return of betrothal presents; claiming for solatium for severing relations between concubine and master and other cases concerning matters between man and woman.

The cases for which conciliation is made possible are as follows;

A) Domestic Relation Cases to be Disposed of either by Adjudgment or Conciliation (Law 17) (Cases class "B"):

(1) Cases Prescribed in the Civil Code.

a) Cohabitation of husband and wife and disposition concerning mutual assistance between husband and wife. (Art. 752)

b) Change in administrator due to the property contract between husband and wife and the division of their common property. (Art. 758, items 2, 3)

c) Divisional payment of expenses accrued from marriage. (Art. 760)

d) Designation of the guardian of a child and other disposition concerning the guardianship of the child in the case of annulment of marriage or divorce. (Art. 766–1, 3; Arts. 749 & 771)

e) Disposition concerning the division of property in the case of annulment of marriage or divorce. (Art. 768–2; 749, 771)

f) Annulment of marriage, divorce, and designation of the successor to ownership of genealogy, altar and grave of the family in the case of termination of blood relation due to the expressed will of the surviving spouse or due to the restoration of the surname of the surviving spouse. (769–2, 751–2, 749, 771)

g) Designation of the guardian of a child and other disposition concerning guardianship in the case of acknowledgment of the child. (788, 766–1, 2)

h) Designation of successor to the ownership of genealogy, altar and grave of the family in the case of cancellation of adoption of adopted child or divorce. (808–2, 817, 769)

i) Designation or change of the person exercising parental power. (819–5, 6)

j) Disposition concerning the support of family members or relatives. (877 to 880 incl.)
k) Disinheritance of presumptive successor and its revocation. (892 to 894 incl.)
l) Designation of successor to the ownership of genealogy, altar and grave of the family in the case of the successor. (892–2)
m) Disposition concerning the division of estate. (907–2, 3).
n) Distribution of property after the enforcement of the Japanese Constitution in the case of annulment of marriage or divorce which was effected before the enforcement of the Civil Code. (Supp. R. 20 and Art. 768–1 C.C)
o) Designation or change of the person exercising the parental power in case where the parental power of a child is exercised jointly by father and mother who were not married at time of enforcement of the New Civil Code (Supp. R. 14–2, 3; Art. 819–6 C.C.)
p) Designation or change of a decree concerning the support of family members or relatives before the enforcement of the New Civil Code. (Supp. R. 24; Art. 880 C.C.)
q) Division of property in case where succession to a house had commenced due to annulment of marriage of adopted husband or divorce of adopted husband or cancellation of adoption of an adopted child, before the Law of Emergency Measures for the Civil Law was put into effect and where there is not an heir to the house at time of enforcement of the New Civil Code. (Supp. R. 27, 25–1 proviso, 28, 27–2)
r) Disposition concerning the inherited property in case where regarding the person who was a member of a house by marriage entering into the house from another house and was the head of the house at time of enforcement of the Law of Emergency Measures for the Civil Code was put into force and there is a heir stepchild in the house. (Supp. Rs. 26–2, 27–2)
s) Division of inherited property in case where succession to a house has commenced due to death of the head of the house after the date of enforcement of the Constitution and there are joint successors prescribed in the New Civil Code. (Supp. R. 27–2)
t) Division of property in case where the person, who was the head of a house at time of enforcement of the Law of Emergency Measures for the Civil Law, has changed his or her surname due to the annulment of marriage, divorce, cancellation or dissolution of adoption of an adopted child after the enforcement of the said Law. (Supp. Rs. 28, 27–2)
u) Division of inherited property as to the succession of estate which

commenced before the enforcement of the Law of Emergency Measures for the Civil Code. (Supp. R. 32; Art. 907–2, 3 C.C).

(2) Cases Prescribed in the Bankruptcy Law.

Change of administrator due to the property contract between husband and wife and the division of common properties. (B.L. 68–1, C.C. 758–2, 3)

(3) Cases Prescribed in the Livelihood Protection Law.

Decision on the amount of payment by the person held responsible for the support of family members or relatives. (L.P.L. Spec. 10–5)

B) Domestic Relations Cases to be Disposed of by Conciliation Only.

Cases concerning all domestic matters other than "A" and "B" adjudgment cases (Law 17) are as follows:

Divorce, cancellation of adoption of a child, invalidity of marriage, annulment of marriage, invalidity of agreement divorce, annulment of agreement divorce, case for determining father, disapproval of legitimate child, acknowledgment cases, invalidity of acknowledgment, cancellation of acknowledgment, invalidity of adoption of an adopted child, cancellation of adoption of child, invalidity of dissolution of agreement adoption, cancellation of dissolution of agreement adoption, confirmation of existence of family relations, non-performance of marriage previously engaged, cohabitation or separation living of parents and child, transfer of infant for upbringing, recovery of succession, reduction of legal shares in legacy, claim for solatium for non-performance of marriage previously engaged, claim for solatium for severing relations between man and woman, return of betrothal presents, lending and borrowing of money or leasehold land and leased buildings between relations.

2) Jurisdiction Based on Land. (The Court to which Application is Made).

Cases of conciliation shall be under the jurisdiction of the Court at the place of domicile of the opponent or the place determined by agreement of both parties. (Reg. 129). Conciliation on the spot may also be arranged as a method of disposition for the case concerning parties whose places of domicile are far apart. However, the Family Court may, if it is found necessary, transfer a case under its own jurisdiction to another Court, or may, when it is deemed proper, dispose of the case falling under the jurisdiction of another Court by itself. (Reg. 4). Even in this case, the Court may adjudge any absentees to pay non-penal fines.

In case where jurisdiction is to be decided according to the place of domicile, the following shall apply: "Place of domicile is not in Japan" or "Place of domicile in Japan is not known" shall be the place of residence (in Japan); when the place of residence does not exist or it is not known the last place of domicile (in Japan) shall apply; and when the last place of domicile does not exist or is not known the Court in the place where the property exists or designated by the Supreme Court (According to the Supreme Court regulation No. 18 of Dec. 29, 1947, the place so designated is Tokyo Metropolis) shall be the competent Court. (Code of Non-contentious Civil Procedures 2). In case where the Court in the place in which succession was commenced is the competent court, the above shall apply even when succession was commenced in a foreign country.

3) District of Jurisdiction of the Tokyo Family Court.
The standard for the district of jurisdiction of the Tokyo Family Court is the same as the administrative divisions of Tokyo Metropolis. Cases falling under the jurisdiction of the Summary Courts in the cities of Hachioji, Tachikawa, Musashino, Awome and Itsudaichi are handled by the Hachioji Branch of the Tokyo Family Court, and the Main Office handles the cases in other districts of Tokyo Metropolis. From this year a detached office of Tokyo Family Court was established in Izu Oshima where cases falling under the jurisdiction of the Summary Courts in Oshima, Niijima and Hachijojima will be handled.

Section 2. Procedures.

52. Procedures for Domestic Matters Conciliation.

1) Application for Conciliation.
The procedures for conciliation are commenced by the application of a party and proceed upon the designation of the date of conciliation. Applications may be laid down in writing or orally, and in a written application the following items must be mentioned:

a) Permanent domicile, residence and full name of applicant and the opponent.
b) Gist of application and details of a conciliation desired.
c) Actual circumstances and contents of the case and its progress.

In the case of an oral application a party must tell the above-cited necessary items in the presence of a clerk of the Court who will draw up a protocol. The original or a copy or an abstract of census register and other documental evidence must be presented at the same time. (Reg. 2, 3)

2) Procedures for Conciliation.
Conciliation is, as a rule, to be conducted by the Conciliation Commis-

sion. A single judge of domestic matters in the Court may execute conciliation, which, however, should be avoided. (Law 3)

A) Conciliation by the Conciliation Commission.

(1) Place of Conciliation.

Conciliation is usually effected in the Court, but may be done at a suitable place out of the Court according to the circumstances of the case, namely, "conciliation on the spot." (Reg. 132)

(2) The Commissioners may order the measures deemed necessary for conciliation before entering in conciliation. (Reg. 133). Utilization of this rule is desirable, but there is no rules to support its execution. Some basic procedures as forcible as provisionary attachment prescribed in the Code of Civil Procedure ought to be set forth in this connection.

(3) The judge presides over conciliation proceedings before the Commission, (Reg. 134) and appointment and change of conciliation date and taking evidence are made by his instructions.

(4) A resolution of Conciliation Commission is adopted by the opinion of majority of commissioners. If the opinion of pros and cons is equally divided, the judge makes decision. (Reg. 135)

(5) Deliberations of the Conciliation Commission are not open to public. (Reg. 136)

(6) The Commission has power to permit or disapprove the presence of a party's representative or assistant under special circumstances. (Reg. 137)

(7) The Commission has on its own motion to inquire the facts and take evidence which it deems necessary. The Commission may requisition another Court of Domestic Relations to inquire the facts or to take evidence. In taking evidence the provisions of the Civil Procedure are applied. (Regs. 7, 137)

(8) The Commission may requisition necessary inquiries to the government agencies or public offices or any other person deemed proper or demand the necessary report as to deposit money, trust property, income or other data of interested parties to a bank, trust company, employer of interested person or other person. (Regs. 8, 137)

It has resently been decided to set up Investigators whose duty is to investigate data in the course of adjudgment and conciliation and also the actual condition after the completion of the proceedings.

(9) Procedures necessary for requisition and demand referred to in the preceding items (7) and (8) shall be taken by the clerk of the Court under the direction of the judge.

(10) Witnesses, expert witnesses and persons who are requisitioned inquiries or demanded reports shall, otherwise provided, be given

travelling expenses, daily allowance, charges for lodging and other expenses. (Reg. 9).

(11) Preparation and Omission of Records.

As regards proceedings in the Court a clerk shall draw up a protocol, but this shall be omitted in cases where the judge recognized it unnecessary. (Reg. 10).

(12) Transfer of Proceedings.

If an applicant is unable to continue the proceedings owing to death, loss of capacity or other reason, a person who has capacity to apply for taking over such proceedings in accordance with laws and ordinances may make application for it. (Regs. 15, 131).

(13) Participation of Interested Persons.

A person interested in the result of conciliation may, by permission of a Court or Conciliation Commission, participate in the proceedings of conciliation. (Regs. 14, 131). In the conciliation terms no third person should be caused to make any presentation. In this case, such third person must be shown as a party or a person interested in the case in all documents.

(14) Inspection of Records and Delivery of Copy of Papers.

A person interested in the case may, with the permission of the Court, inspect or take copy of the records, or receive from a clerk of the Court an authenticated copy, a copy or an extract of record or a certificate relating to the case. In order to take the above procedure after a case is concluded, however, a party must pay the fees as otherwise provided. (Reg. 12).

(15) Expenses and Party who Pays Them.

The expenses of inquiring facts, taking evidence, summons, notification or other necessary disposition shall be advanced by the National Treasury. But the Court may cause a party to prepay them concerning the acts which require expenses. (Reg. 11). As to the method of recovery of the said advance, it is not clearly provided in the Government Accounting. A certain legislation will be required, I think, in which a party who is too poor to pay them could apply to the Family Court for the exemption from the payment of such expenses.

For the application of conciliation a party is required to pay a fee of thirty (30) yen per case, in revenue stamp, to the Court as regards the adjudgment of a case class "B" and a case for which conciliation only is applied. The final party who pays the expenses shall be decided at the discretion of the Court or the Conciliation Commission. (Non-Contentious Civil Procedures Law 26, etc.).

(16) Refusal of Conciliation.

In cases where the Commission considers that the case is not suitable for conciliation in view of its nature, or that a party applies for conciliation without sufficient reason for the unjust purpose, it may not take the trouble of the conciliation (Reg. 138). In this case, I think, we ought to prepare a protocol to the effect that no conciliation is made.

(17) The Court shall give notice to parties without delay when it is adjudged that conciliation is unsuccessful and a decree is not rendered, or a decree loses its effect by the raise of objection (Reg. 141).

(18) When only one Commissioner was present on the conciliation day and an agreement was reached between the parties, it is advisable to form a regular commission with other commissioners supplemented.

B) Conciliation Undertaken by One Judge.

In case where a judge makes conciliation alone, the provisions concerning spot conciliation (132), measures taken prior to conciliation (133), rejection of conciliation for improper and abusive application (138), and notification to parties (141) shall correspondingly apply (Reg. 142).

Section 3. Validity.

53. Validity of Domestic Matters Conciliation. When an agreement is made between the parties in conciliation and it is entered in a protocol, the conciliation is deemed to have been formed and such record shall have the same validity as the final decree. The Conciliation Commission shall, when such agreement or consent is recorded in a protocol, immediately sign the protocol. As to the matter prescribed in Art. 9–1 of the Law hereof, it has the same binding effect as a final decree. (Art. 21–1). For instance, when a conciliation for divorce is made it is legally valid. Even when the opponent does not sign a report of divorce, the divorce will be valid when a copy of such conciliation protocol is attached to the report. It is, however, illegal in this case if one submits a report on agreement divorce instead of the conciliation divorce.

Such being the case, the validity as mentioned above shall be nullified on the agreement concerning the conciliation degrees cited hereunder (Law 21–2), because objection may be raised against conciliation decree. (Law 25–1). The reason why we say that it has the same effect as a final decree is that no virtual validity could be enforced on matters of conciliation.

It is true that inasmuch as a successful conciliation has validity same as a final decree it is possible to enforce it in accordance with provision of compulsory execution prescribed in the Code of Civil

Procedure, but in view of the special character of the domestic matters conciliation it is advisable, as the principle of law, to establish a special system of legal enforcement. As to the right to claim for support of family members or relatives, we think it necessary to lay down provisions to allow the application of general preferential rights. If there was no agreement reached on a part of the case at issue in conciliation, it is sufficient to mention the facts in the conciliation terms.

Any miscalculations, clerical arrors or any other similar apparent mistakes in the conciliation terms could be corrected and decided by applying correspondingly the provision of Art. 194 of the Code of Procedure. A protocol of the succesful conciliation is now usually sent to the parties upon their request, but it is advisable to change the system so as to send it by the authority of the Court for in doing so it will be more effective to secure the performance of conciliation terms.

Section 4. Special Adjudgment in Conciliation.

54. Special Adjudgments.

1) Kinds and Procedures.

The Law for Adjudgment of Domestic Matters approves the two cases of adjudgment to be made in conciliation.

A) Conciliation Adjudgment (Law 23).

(1) Kinds of the cases are the following seven and no more:

(*a*) Invalidity or annulment of marriage or adoption of child; (*b*) invalidity or cancellation of agreement divorce and dissolution of adoptive relations; (*c*) acknowledgments; (*d*) invalidity or cancellation of acknowledgment; (*e*) case to determine the father of a child born to a woman who remarried before six (6) months have not elapsed after the date on which her previous marriage was dissolved or canceled gave birth to the child within 200 days from the date of her remarriage after elapse of 300 days from the date of dissolution or cancellation of her previous marriage; (*f*) disapproval of a heir child; (*g*) confirmation of existence of family relations. (When the parents who are not real parent on census register have died, application may be made for confirmation as to the existence of parent and child relations between the child and its natural parents).

(2) Conciliation by the Conciliation Commission is only permissible.

(3) Essential conditions are: (*a*) Nothing disputable exists as to the cause of the case; (*b*) an agreement has been made between the parties; (*c*) inquiries have been conducted by authority; (*d*)

opinion of commissioners is to be heard; (*e*) agreement must be deemed just and proper for settlement of the case.

(4) If the above conditions are fulfilled the Court may make a proper adjudgment conforming to the agreement.

(5) When the Court does not make any adjudgment, (e.g., in the case of determining father when the type of blood does not conform to the statement of agreement) the Court shall notify the parties of the facts without delay. (Reg. 141)

B) Adjudgment of Compulsory Conciliation (Law 24–1).

(1) Kinds of the cases: applicable to all cases other than those adjudgment cases prescribed in Art. 9, par. 1, class "B" of the Law hereof.

(2) Conciliation by the Commission is only permissible.

(3) Conditions: (*a*) Though the conciliation is unsuccessful, the dispute is not too serious or is promising to be settled amicably by compulsory conciliation without any objection raised; (*b*) the Commissioner's opinion is to be heard; (*c*) fair and proper deliberations be given for the parties; (*d*) consideration be given to all circumstances involved; (*e*) not contrary to the wishes expressed by both parties.

(4) The Court may adjudge divorce, dissolution of adoptive relations and other necessary adjudgments. In this decree the presentation of pecuniary payment or other properties can be ordered.

(5) As stated above, compulsory conciliation cannot be made as to the so-called adjudgment cases class "B", but if the cases class "B" proved unsuccessful it is regarded that an application for adjudgment was made at the time when conciliation was applied for. (Law 26)

(6) When the Court does not make compulsory conciliation, it shall notify, without delay, the parties to that effect.

2) Validity of Special Adjudgment.

The validity of the above-cited two kinds of special adjudgment is extremely meagre and weak. If a party raises objection to the Court within two weeks counting from the day on which he received the notice of decree, (Law Reg. 139) the validity of such decree is lost. (Law 25–1, 2). The person who has the right to raise objection is a party or an interested person in the case of compulsory conciliation, while in the case of adjudgment by conciliation, it is limited to an interested person. It is because the party or the judge has made an agreement correspondent to a decree. A person who raised an objection may make an immediate complaint against decree to dismiss the raise of the objection. (Reg. 140). If conciliation is unsuccessful and a decree loses its effect the Court shall give notice to that effect to the parties without delay. (Reg. 141). To my thinking, as this provision of Art. 25 of the

Law hereof not only obstructs the formation of agreement in conciliation, but jeopardises the dignity of a Court, it is advisable that the method of submitting complaint be revised so as to cause the case to be transferred, upon the raise of an objection, to the Civil Procedure as pendency of an action.

Section 5. Notification to Census Registrar.

55. Notice to the Census Registrar.
In case where conciliation is concluded with respect to divorce, dissoluation of adoptive relation or other matters which require application for or correction of the family register or decree mentioned in any of Art. 23 or 24, par. 1 of the Law hereof becomes binding, the Court, without delay, gives notice to that effect to the person who handles the family register at the place of the registered locality of the party of the case. (Reg. 143). The matters concerning the above ruling are: (1) Divorce or dissolution of adoptive relation by conciliation; (2) invalidity and annulment of marriage; (3) Invalidity and revocation of divorce; (4) designation of parental power; (5) change of person exercising the parental power; (6) invalidity and cancellation of adoption of child; (7) invalidity and cancellation of dissolution of adoptive relation; (8) acknowledgment and invalidity and cancellation thereof; (9) disapproval of heir child; (10) revocation of presumptive successor.

Section 6. Transfer of Conciliation and Adjudgment.

56. Relation between Conciliation and Adjudgment.

1) As regards the so-called cases class "B" the applicant may choose at his discretion either adjudgment or conciliation. The Court also submits such class "B" adjudgment cases to conciliation any time. (Law II)

2) In cases where conciliation is applied for in respect of a case under proceedings of adjudgment or where a case is submitted to conciliation, the proceedings of adjudgment may be suspended until conciliation is concluded. (Reg. 20)

3) Conciliation of cases class "B" is unsuccessful, it is presumed that an adjudgment has been applied at the time of the conciliation.

Section 7. Conciliation Priority Principle.

57. Relation between Conciliation and Lawsuit.

1) Conciliation priority principle. In order to bring an action in

respect of the cases for which conciliation can be made, it is necessary to apply first for the conciliation of the Family Court. (Law 18–1)

2) In cases where an action is brought without applying for conciliation in respect of the cases mentioned in the preceding paragraph, the Court shall submit the case to the conciliation of the Family Court unless the Court deems it improper to submit it to conciliation. (Law 18–2)

3) In case where a case for conciliation can be made is pending as a suit in a Court, the Court may send it any time *ex officio* to the Family Court for conciliation. (Law 19). The purpose of the preceding three provisions in based on the principle of conciliation priority. In cases where the conciliation is unsuccessful and a decree of conciliation or compulsory conciliation is not rendered, or a decree loses its effect, if a party has brought an action within two weeks from the day on which he received such notice, it is deemed that such action has been brought retroactively at the time of applying for conciliation. This procedure will produce a good effect as to the prescription or the term of a suit.

Section 8. Penal Provisions.

58. Penalties.

1) Violation of Obligation to Enter Appearance. (Law 27)
If a person interested in a case for which summons was served by the Family Court or the Conciliation Commission neglects to appear without reasonable causes, the Court may fine a non-penal fine not exceeding five hundred (500) yen. (Law 27). In the Civil Affairs Mediation Law the corresponding fine is prescribed not to exceed three thousand (3,000) yen (Art. 21), and it is necessary to fix the amount similarly in the conciliation of domestic matters.

With regard to the procedure and the method of execution for the fine, there is no provision in the Law of Adjudgment of Domestic Matters or the Rules thereof. Accordingly, as a general rule for non-penal fines are applied the supplementary provisions of the Law of Procedure for Non-Contentious Matters (207 to 208–2): (*a*) Decisions on fines are to be made with a decree with reason and an immediate complaint may be made against this decree. The term of such complaint is two weeks, (Rule 14); (*b*) Before a decree is made the statement of the party must be heard. Without hearing the opinion of the party the Court may adjudge a decree, but when an objection is raised a re-adjudgment is required; (*c*) For the judge the public procurator's opinion must be heard; (*d*) Punishment of non-penal fines is executed by the order of a public procurator.

2) Offense against Duty to Keep Secrecy. (Law 28)
If and when a person who is or was a conciliation commissioner has disclosed, without good reason, the progress of a conference, and the opinion or number of opinions of judges or commissioners, he is liable to a penalty not exceeding one thousand (1.000) yen. (Law 28). The same provisions shall apply against the councillors.

3) Offense against Disclosure of Secrets. (Law 29)
A councillor, a conciliation commissioner, or a person who held a post of this duty has disclosed, without good reason, the secrets of persons whom he was able to be acquainted with by handling his duty, is liable to penal servitude not exceeding six (6) months or a penalty not exceeding three thousand (3,000) yen.

GPSR Compliance

The European Union's (EU) General Product Safety Regulation (GPSR) is a set of rules that requires consumer products to be safe and our obligations to ensure this.

If you have any concerns about our products, you can contact us on ProductSafety@springernature.com

In case Publisher is established outside the EU, the EU authorized representative is:

Springer Nature Customer Service Center GmbH
Europaplatz 3
69115 Heidelberg, Germany

Batch number: 10843651

Printed by Printforce, the Netherlands